like a perhaps hand

poems by

Peter McNamara

for Ed —
love + friendship always
                    Peter

. . . carefully
moving a perhaps
fraction of flower here placing
an inch of air there)and
without breaking anything.

—e.e. cummings

This book is made possible through the *Richard Walser and Bernice Kelley Harris Fund* of the Hanes Charitable Lead Trust

Library of Congress Cataloging-in-Publication Data

McNamara, Peter. Like a Perhaps Hand / Peter McNamara—
Laurinburg, NC / St. Andrews College Press
I. McNamara, Peter II. Title

St. Andrews College Press
1700 Dogwood Mile
Laurinburg, NC 28352

ISBN: 1-879934-67-1

Cover Photo: Peter McNamara
Author Photo: John Paul McNamara

Typeset in Arial

acknowledgements

A number of these poems appeared (sometimes in different form) in the following publications: *American Poets & Poetry, Atlanta Review, Chelsea, Denver Quarterly, Pheonix, Polyphon,* and *Seneca Review.*

I wish to express my appreciation to Ron Bayes for his shrewd eye and unfailing support.

contents

Mme. Manet at Bellevue (1880)

I sit as he has posed me:
hat brim shading my jawline,
arms of the bentwood chair
I studiedly don't back against
gauging a precise effect.
And as Edouard works
enigmatic whorls in *plein air*
I strike my own enigma—
mystery in a straw hat—
shadowed in thought
of his invention, more
enigmatic than mirage,

perhaps, to idle passersby—
footfalls on tine-raked gravel
displacing the Gallic order.
What might a stroller see
if he should raise his eyes?
A bourgeois in dappled light?
Primness beneath a veil?
And what do I see?
Trim shoes and trouser cuffs.
Invention conveys only so much
Of enigma as we would share.
Or as we dare.

Tyn Church, Prague

Light angles off through quires of gray;
Failing, it fails the reach of hope.
The Old Town Square stoops beneath
Canceled sun, impervious to change:
Too many expectations balked,
Too many skirmishes of faith. Buildings
Seem caught between new-painted pride
And resignation. The astronomical clock
Chimes its plodding tourist-turn
More out of custom than conviction.
I find myself wanting a sliver of light—
But I might better recall the past than
To turn to Tyn Church, long walled out
By commerce, black towers craning for a
Glimpse into the Square. Through a dim,
Dust-chalked elbowway the Church gasps
Soot and exhaustion. A few pinched
Derelicts shadow its great door
And, inside, haunt its aisles. What might
They scour for in this house of damp—
Even whose saints appear ready to flee—
Where Hussites put the old faith to rout,
Then had their own cup spilt, melted
To forge a Virgin's crown? A graying
Icon, now only its ghosts recall
Crusades to right a toppling world.

              .   .   .

Yet there, from its dark corners—listen:
A tapping, faint but persistent,
From someone at their task to beat back time,
Flake ages of hosannas from the stone,
Repoint its grace. Perhaps the great Corpus
Looming above the nave has caught
A glint of light: is that the warmth of sun
Across its tracery? Even the motes
Seem alive a moment in the closeness
And cold. Might Epiphany lurk
At the vestibule, peering into gloom?

Windows on Florence

At just five a.m. the water wagon
Shrills morning in cramped streets
As full-throated as a town crier,
Fanning grime toward sluices,
Settling dust. Light detonates,
Yellowing mauve air by instants.

Early swifts torque above roofs;
Gouaches of stifled July glance
Cadmium fire off stucco across
Belle Donne through our windows.
Church bells begin to prowl and poke
Around corners, then shy away.

Unflinching eight o'clock conducts
First shopkeepers to the street:
The newslady with the quiet smile,
Mona Lisa of tabloids, who takes in
The stir from her shadowed recess,
Greeting every familiar passer-by;

The laundry woman who presses
White hours into evening through her
Window on fleeting day; the couple
Whose trattoria air mounts our
Stairwell at mid-morning, and whose
Food sustains us often of a night.

Above the street open shutters exploit
Morning's brevity. The young mother
Leans on the sill, then lifts her toddler
To look as her older boy fulcrums it,
Hovering in air. Two windows over
An old man strains for freshness,

Already overlaid with heat. At the
Upper corner an old woman perches,
Eyes darting toward color and run
Where streets spill for Via Tornabuoni,
From which we turn for the museums,
Shops, and street markets' vibrancy.

We draw our shutters on sunslash,

Then wind down the still-cool stairwell.
Past our street door cacophany
Carries us up Via Calzaiuoli to the
Piazza del Duomo, where Florentine
Adolescents idle through each day:

Not the keen-eyed Florentine youth
Who built Tuscany's merchant towns,
Now in tight knots they crowd beneath
The Duomo's cramped geometries—
Inlays of soft green, white and red—
Their eyes flicking to tourists' eyes.

Where are the sparks of the Medici
Who built dreams which they could
Command, raised beauty by their wills
To civic virtue, and patronized visions—
Earthly, ethereal—Botticelli's Venus,
Ghiberti's Gates of Paradise?

*   *   *   *   *

At our midafternoon return windows
Are eyes shuttered against the heat.
One by one, just at six, families begin
To look out again on softening angles.
The young husband slicks back his hair,
Shower-wet after his love-making;

The old man putters at his sink
To cull produce for his frugal meal;
The family which bathes each night
In the light of World Cup images
Begins to stir. Their teenagers grab
A soccer ball and head for the street.

All around Tuscans turn to families,
To joy; light shades to dark, music
Resounds, laughter echoes; life is
Refleshed with a Florentine verve.
The bright-lit Piazza Maria Novella
Alters its tempo as young people—

8

Couples, groups—lounge on the grass
And stroll to the gelateria. Night
Gathers in windows: the old woman
Shakes her tablecloth over the street,
The young parents share a last glass
Of wine, a refreshing quiet moment.

The last diners' laughter caroms upward,
Wringing the air. Loud shouts and leaps
Across signal a World Cup win: dark
Turns shrill with jubilant car horns, flags
Flap from sky roofs, and joyous fans
Careen beneath windows on Florence.

Sentinels: Liscannor

(County Clare, Ireland)

Clay roads perennial with wet
Yawn around axles; ruts spider
Gray-green peatscapes. The few
Roofless cottages tilt toward sloughs,
Unbaked scones on blackened sheets.
Grimaced over by inhospitable gray
The land echoes its emptiness; earth
Itself breeds threat. Still, stout walls
Assert the claims of withered life.

Stones are damp now, hearths dark
With sentinels' memories. In mantels
Families incised intent; now grass
Tufts in chimneys, roughcast flakes
Away, and turf thrives where roofslates
Held truce with rain. Above, a hawk
Rides an updraft; out a window hole
Hills overlaid with faults and shifts
Of shale drink in a moment's sun.

The winds blew fiercely, bit and tore.
Sheltered from blow, potato plants
Glinted green warmth. The crop made.
Failed. Rotted in the ground. One year
Wavered to another—another
Failed crop, and death everywhere.
As bloodless till-keepers set down
Profit and loss, the poor were set down
To famine roads far from their hearths.

Other boots rang on gangways and
Looked from the land they loved, looked
Into mystery in a slow-march not music,
Not daring: with hope beyond hope.
Their abandoned hearths are strewn
With the straw of nest-builders;
Yet they stand sentinel in the west,
Where roads hunger to devour
And cast wet shadows against light.

Remorseless Sun

July sun crisps in deep-fry haze.
We press on across Ponte Trinita,
Loosed from familiar routine, then
Falter in the fiery Florentine air.
Below us the Arno churns, turgid ochre,
While swallows drop down sky.

Impasto glints off the river's swell—
Sinewy shoulders roil its banks until
They next rampage, bolting
Their confines to maraud the streets
And square—as sudden, as resistless
As the impulse for art's Renaissance.

Thoughts of the lunch we'd set out for
Waver in stifling air; still we plod on,
Hesitant to give in to our wilting wills.
South of the Arno, streets constrict:
Stucco walls radiate heat, spilling us
Single file into cobblestoned streets.

We slow, window shop half-heartedly,
Zig-zagging to any oasis of shadow.
Molten light dapples fretwork canopies;
Pollen silts from ovations of plane trees
Which frame Piazza Santo Spirito,
Drooping in merciless noontime glare

Beneath which alfresco cafés stifle.
The Piazza poaches as dispirited
Sparrows hop and peck—more out of
Instinct than appetite. Palazzi facades
Fling light-alleys toward the cafés. We
Sit at a familiar favorite; two women

Choose a table nearby, one tucking a
Golden cocker puppy, secure on his lead,
Beneath their feet. Agitated by the heat,
Caught in the hour's lassitude—our few
Words strained through ennui—we order
By rote, chilled *vino bianco* first, little

Interested in food. A baked gust billows
At us, overbears us. The chilled *bianco*
Proves soporific in the heat; our thoughts
Drift and we scarcely notice a young man
Who greets the women, his frisking dog

Rousting the puppy beneath the table.
The man proposes that they let their
Dogs off-lead. Our *risotti di mare* arrive,
Embryo-pink squid snuffing our appetites.
Beyond our vision the dogs sweep

Widening arcs. As the young man
Chats up the women, we push aside
Half-eaten plates and decant the last wine
From our carafe. The heat thickens,
Assuming an audible buzz—a moped's
Shrill whine grating the smothered air.

A teenaged couple—laughing, engrossed—
Rides into the square; then skitters,
Braking in view of our tables. The wine
Sears my throat as I make out a tangle—
The puppy's still-pulsing copper—under
The moped's wheels. Sunstrike springs

Shock in rivulets of sweat; in the square,
Flurried concern, the body gently lifted—
Attended by head-shaking, loud dismay.
The young man cradles the puppy, glances
Anxiously about as muted life, shivering,
Leaks away under remorseless sun.

Sunset: Pont Sully

Behind us allées of Ile Sainte-Louis
Trail last faint whispers through the dark;
After-images in humid June fade
Like first dreams in a restless night.
We cross from shadow. Pont Sully
Glows blood orange; spill from sun
Touched down ignites the Seine,
Sets its current on a crimson boil.
We strike out into angled mazes
Free as riverflow, turning dead ends
To chance explorations, vivid tableaux—
Yet strange as spacewalks to small stars
Set in impenetrable, gathered dark.
A couple false turnings—then we come
Right in Rue Sainte-Antoine, quiet
Culs-de-sac unraveling in neon
Irruptions of car horns, of anxious
People snatching at dying day.
Prometheus soars the Marais' hub
Where neon cafes elbow for patronage
As skaters punk its paved interstices.

Cumnor, Oxfordshire

Low hills scud and canter
Across an arc of fields;
The sky hangs static, clouds
Stuck up like cotton-wool.
Rapeseed brims and tumbles
Behind snarls of wild rose
And birds strung, wire-hung,
Angle into a slight lift.
Laburnums cascade yellow
Onto chestnut's massed tapers;
Everywhere air is buoyed
By a freshness of lilacs.
As the breeze stirs shadows,
Veils of light sport in fields,
Thatched cottages puff pipes
And the Norman tower, uncloyed,
Surveys it all again—grasses
Teeming for the mower, dense
Tangles damp against its blade.

Pablo Neruda: from *Cien sonetos de amor*

VIII

If your eyes hadn't glints of the moon,
of daylit clay, of work and fire,
if, even curbed, you weren't agile as air,
like an amber week,

like the yellow moment
when autumn trails through vines,
the bread the fragrant moon kneads
scattering flour through the sky,

oh, lover, I could not love you so!
In your embrace I hold all that exists—
sand, time, the rain-drenched tree—

all that lives so that I may live:
without roving I can see everything:
in your life I see all life.

XXVII

Naked, you are as unadorned as your hand—
lithe, earthy, slight, rounded, diaphanous—
marked by moonlines, appleways;
naked, you are slender as unhusked wheat.

Naked, you are blue as the Cuban night,
comet trails and stars in your hair;
naked, you are stunning and luminous
as summer light in a golden church.

Naked, you are as small as your fingernail:
curved, delicate, rosy as daybreak;
and you enter the subterranean world

as through a long tunnel of labors and travails:
your clarity muted, obscured, uncloaks itself—
and you reappear, as unadorned as your hand.

LXIX

Without you, being would perhaps not be being—
without you gliding, cutting through midday
like a sky-blue flower, strolling evening
through mist and bricks,

without the light you carry in your hand,
whose glow others perhaps do not see,
which perhaps no one sees waxing
like the red opening of a rose,

in short without your being, your sudden
stirring, coming to know my life—
flash of rosebush, wheat in wind—

and since then, I am because you are,
since then, I and you are we,
and through love, I and you, we shall be.

Light Pools: Vermont

1

Light pools cluster like golden grapes
Across the Persian carpet; my eyes
Are drawn to the bay window—to
Rain-slicked maples—as shuttered sun
Freeze-frames clearing air. Time
Trickles sorbet tartness along
My nerves, suspends idle thought
In its web; across the living room
My aunt knits, her needles ticking
Instants to memory. Thought nets a
Small catch at such quiet moments,
Fading to rotogravure with each tick,
Each loop of her deft fingers knotting
Time more enduringly than words.

2

I take the spiral steps two at a time,
At the head of the stairs pry loose
The stubborn hook on the attic door;
It sags inward, jams on floorboards.
Within, a lost planet catches me
In a time-warp; motes of faded hours
Sift through stifled dormer light, and
Slow to suspension in tired air;
Baked dust emits a slow-charred tang.
Under eaves disjointed dolls, rusted
Tinware, an abandoned trousseau—
Finery for some forgotten soiree
Grimed with ages of its jilted dignity—
Spill like lava from stained boxes.

3

Sifting cold ash I recollect old tales
Of rum runners' sojourns en route
To New York—"hottest party house
From Montreal to Albany." Dustballs
Beneath settees, ghost dancers, stir
Like figures on an old town clock—
But more lithe and, though pale, more
Proximate: the room billows skirts.
Fades. So dispiriting late November:
Shuttered, alone, with only a teacup's
Suffusion to warm. Cleat-scarred floors
Score summers past; faint echoes raise
Endless rounds of lunch, now done.
The old house waits, expectant.

Green Parrots

Green parrots screech and skitter
Through wine-bright winter skies
To thinning oaks, to sidle down
Each limb—arthritic old men—
Pecking mites from moss tufts.
Their sharp, proprietary shrieks
Pierce as they soar day's close;
Their wings veer furious darts
Disdaining—it seems—the tropic lift
Which kites pelicans, ballasted
With a day's catch, toward sunset.
Vaunting semaphores, they flash
Crisp green, spiced marmalade,
Stair-stepping air to clear clouds
Above which they may glimpse
Through gaps the tangled past,
Undrained marshes of memory.
* * *

O Florida, O pillaged tropic
Shadowed in bartered mystery,
Shrouded in tendrilled vine,
Turgid with quaking earth—how
Did you face your defamation?
* * *

In mangrove swamps palm fronds
Rattle; from tall pines, mosses
Toast in wine-bright air. Swamp's
Heart pulses slow life; its sluggish
Beat floats its cargoes—teeming,
Decaying, monstrous, minuscule.
Gators, content to surf the current,
Suffer small birds to root insects
From their heads and backs. Above,
Parrots screech their raucous joy.
No creature's peace is troubled
Yet by specters of strip malls,
Houses elbowing the shore,
The marshes denuded, drained.
Sun doesn't frown through smog.
Parrots dart the swamp, then glide
Toward trees to gorge abundance.

Hawkwing and Helix

This hawk-bright day struck off
Sillion, this stealthy skate of wing:
Sunlight's caught mischief candled
In crooks of trees; leaves flared
Fierce green, except where faded
Palm fronds trail yellow streamers,
Past's abstractions; and all well
In an instant—*the beauty of an old
Indian woman playing dominoes
With a chicken.* The earth, ducks'
Slow parables rippling lakeflash,
And spirits sore with loss caught
In an instant's clarity refract the
Transitory shadows of happiness
No one evades. At the blue verge
Of joy's endurance double helixes
Menace crystal light—to elbow its
Carnival from the image theatre
And drain its receding wellspring.

Koan of Communion

Stiff green gusts plump pillow waves.
Children shriek as they tumble
In the heavy chop; teens bodysurf,
Weaving their wind-veer grace;
Middle-aged women vaunt in sunhats
And loose caftans which flap and tent.
A small boat runs so low its bobbing sail
Mimics angelfish feeding in the swell.
Joggers strain to ballast against gusts
As a youth in a turquoise T—assumed
Nonchalance—strides through bluster,
His earphones' assertive bass
Counterpointing the Gulf's salt roar.
A windsurfer sleek in black arrives
To take the wind: assembles his sail,
Draws on his bright-colored wetsuit,
Anticipates with an edgy relish
Of adrenaline fear-laced elation—
The rush when rising wind and surf
Weld him to their tempo. Readied,
He anoints his board to exchange vows
With the surf, mounts westering light
To invoke his koan of communion.

Green Lemons

The lemons are still green, but are
Already the size of ripe market fruit;
When they grow golden they'll be
Big as baseballs, as gloating fists.
Blossoms pitched their high sweet
Through February's fragile warmth
Into my bedroom—so seductively—
Scenting my wintery mood, wafting
Don't think to feel a northern beat
In this sub-tropic world. And now
These lemons nod with each stir,
Each breath, dance their sambas
At bent bows' ends, and laugh their
Infectious Latin joy, nudging me—
To ready ice for the bright glasses
And envision chill drops beading,
Then snaking like stealthy lizards
To the pulse of impassioned hearts.

Idling

The scent of bathers in melon light
trails tendrils of sun block;
gusts scale from stifled sky.
Seagulls strut stiff-legged arcs,
and screech to flight at any stir.
Dog-belly sun scratches itself along
the beachfront's splintered glass
while on FM Lou Reed larrups life—
"And Romeo had Juliet,
And Juliet had her Romeo"—
traffic recoils on its own exhaust
and office towers choke on smog.

"It's hard to give a shit these days"
Lou whines, as paperback romances
riffle in the wind. Slubs of Saturday
strewn like scattered sandcastles
reconstitute themselves as Sunday—
flaccid, scarcely daring to breathe;
troughs of Gulf tide grope for shore
too enervated even to crest.
Still, pelicans glide above morning
to snag the Gulf's cold heart,
indifferent as the idlers sweat
night's revels into fish-scale mist.

Annals of Commerce # 2

Thunderheads intimate a backlit sky.
Middle-ground, corn dogs and crushed ice
Strew Clearwater Causeway—"there's widespread
Interest in what our people have done";
Foreground, barnacle-crusted whitewall crumbles:
Scoured still-life with sun-quashed tangerine
And imperturbable gulls—"our mutual fund. . .
Select package of financial instruments";
Background, *Alice* recycles flickering laugh tracks.
Well, I've invested in this runny-melt spread—
Chilis rellenos, a Cuervo Margarita—while
One table over two scammers plot to fleece
Each other—"poised for maximum growth"—if these
Rain clouds don't germinate. Otherwise, both'll
Take a bath: Nature persists, even in a panic,
Its harmonies spherical, not in broken bonds—
Floating free, flaking, falling among gulls.

The Quality of Rain in New York

It seems a thing you had always known,
Something in your blood remembered
Long before you had tasted the salt
Of wisdom, even in sun-flooded June
Lurking to turn summer to autumn
At a whim—elation with sting and slash.

It seems to ferret out your most porous
Chink or gap with dogged persistence,
Seems wetter—more capable of wetting—
Than other rain: hair-drenching wash
Which you shake off in sprays, only
To sponge up yet more tenacious wet
Which gutters from your brow, and spits
Off each thrust gable of your mood.

It spurs a stroll to quickstep hurry home,
A neighbor nudging you—to feel, inhale
More keenly—as it sparks off pavement,
Cascades from pigeoned eaves, pends
Pearls from green tendrils, and snakes
Rivulets across misted windowpanes.

Dying Sun

Even noon's late September sun leaks
Only watery warmth on the Village;
Washed-out pastels parody summer,
Teasing tank-topped hustlers who loiter
West Street, hunkered into stucco
Warmth against bone-chill autumn.
The hustlers are sticking it out, not yet
Ready to relinquish lucrative posts
Along the riverfront's foot and vehicle
Artery, although weak, dilute light
Leaves them shivering, wanting a roost,
Heated space anywhere out of the stiff
Blow starting to kick off the Hudson.
Feet troop by—no one buying—while sharp
Air goads the tank-tops. In minutes
Their number thins, though not one's been
Approached. Quiet overtakes the piers—
Awaits inevitable night prowls' start—
As sun brands its hot disk into Hoboken
And light wicks the Hudson's wavecaps,
Lingering until one last hustler's gone.

Green Hill October

Clouds drape their soiled sheets over
The vertebrae of fleshless hills;
Branches scratch any way for sun,
Abandoned by October's waning light.
Damp probes rock gardens whose
Soil leeches its last warmth. Harvest
Bunting's been furled; the tour buses
Have flown with late September, as if
An internet posting had trumpeted:
"Vermont's denatured; its colors struck!"
The fog flits in, fingers tired old barns,
Cutting the vista to sleet's white noise.

Caught, faltering along a window frame
To spring (unwary) into a snow shower,
You inch feebly across a frozen crank
Puzzling escape, unaware what waits
Beyond your reticulated prison's screen,
Beyond the wood stove's mock summer,
Last warmth you will know; and in your
Blind stumble death's probing finger
Flips you on your back, your wings too
Weak to right you, your season done.
One leg pulses and winter takes you,
Last of all the buzzing life of June.

Fat orange gourds glut the landscape;
At Mach's General Store one pumpkin—
Misshapen as a punch-drunk pug—grins
Gap-toothed, drooling a seed or two.
Robins flock to retreat: veer through
Branches, perch in leafless shrubs,
Peck across brown lawns for the few
Worms which haven't burrowed too deep.
Mach's hearty hot chili, washed down
With British ale, cheers the chill noon
Of workmen and tourists. Pawlet, living
Its way, shrugs off another mud season.

November Onset

The trees wear their November reach—
They roam the sky familiarly
Plucking at its cerise backcloth
As it furls in unpeopling dusk.

Brittle cold: a few last students angle
Across doubt, sprinting stairflights,
Exhaling sharp breaths; light leeches,
Cowling their haste in flinty echoes.

West Philadelphia: a windswept flight
Of starlings, tossed in sheared gusts,
Ripples, lights in green interstices
To worry where next to flock for seed.

Why do such fluid geometries of birds
Court no chaos, whether they furl
Fold upon fold, or dart, or veer at
Acute angles through dim brass air?

Bronze piers arch into peach clabber;
Against the Schuylkill scull-like feet
Pick up the beat, hurling ducks' heavy
Underbellies upward, free of the skim.

A young man sweet talks his cell phone—
A date or deal—his door ajar to the wind;
Houses squint in the sting as November's
Onset slivers sun zests through murk.

29

Surreal November

Uneasy in the cloud-banked damp
Of Florida's surreal November,
Inert sun-seekers glow sulfurous—
Apartment-sized appliances—
Amid a congregation of gulls
Witnessing to the gospel of the breeze.
Pelicans plummet death from the sky
While waves, like unskilled laborers,
Are kept at their task all hours,
Revising history in slow motion.
Odd-lot tourists pitch umbrellas
As their quick children rout the gulls;
One lingerer frets our prospect
To worry a few orts for his craw as
A small boy, fierce with energy,
Tramples a giant sand figure,
His conquest unconditional.
The blonde in the anorexic bikini
Flees along the slick pursued by Furies,
As the giant-slayer—sated—retires
To his victory, and to lunch.
Swept aloft by gusts, the gulls
Shriek homilies in amber light.

Postcard to the Mountain

The shower tiles glint brittle white.
Water cascades warmth down my back,
Plucking at nerves, while camomile
Tincts the clouded steam. But outside
October calls its crisp salute,
And so I'm sending this postcard
To the mountain: I'm speechless; I
Lack wit or trope to express your
Inexpressible shadows, the fire
Of lights that must so soon be snuffed.
And let me say—in glyphs that only
Grope at evanescence—I know
How camera-shy you've turned watching
The depth of your mystery diminished,
Your spectacle's bright dance reduced
To henscratch in a farmyard's dust.
So I'll call upon blood memory
To fix these snapshots on my pulse
Where time cannot distort or dim.

Northeast Kingdom

Shouldery Matisse nudes—jilted
Ages ago by glacial lovers—
The mountains lie quiet before dawn,
Lengths etched against the sky.
First light scatters like a fling
Of seed, then fires their ridgetops,
Threatens to wake the ample-hipped
Odalisques—whose figures pulse
In sleep that salves their loss—
But passes instead to the valley,
Settling in hollows from which it
Lures lake mists to rise cloaking,
Then cleansing the mountains
In showers of gold. Belatedly
They stir, grow taut with grief.
Birches flutter small hand mirrors
In which the earth dons radiance;
Branches cant toward warmth;
Breezes whisper vain consolation
To sleepers roused to pain.

Encounter

I caught your glance—like a
Guitar in a pawnshop window,
One string broken—
Abandoned, purposeless.

Dirty blond hair, lank with
Dejection, half-hid your eyes.
You didn't look at me, I knew—
Who you looked at hadn't come—

I placed a hand on your shoulder;
A shadow lifted your cheekbones.
I gave you dinner, a few bucks,
And you were on your way.

I hope that hope—that shadow—
Followed where you've gone.

Mares'-tail Moon

On the night of the poets' speaking
Mares' tails flick across the moon
Like ephemera of wit before words,
Recapturing half thoughts—black holes
From which genetic codes await capture—
Their dark strands trailing images
As elusive as clouds' moonlit canter.
Writers and listeners gather like
Astronomers to sky discoveries;
The stir sparks recollection's probe
Into space—its lunar backstage—
For uncaught glints, fugitive details
That might fix on the sky's silver salts
The idiom of life—pulsing, fluid—
As of the past reconstituted, lived again:
To brush the moon with textures
Of incident scattered adrift, not lost,
Like starlight, ages after, flooding earth.

Small Elegy

(for Dean X. Johnson)

If he is dead
music
fades at the horizon

dims—must—over
town
If he is dead

song rings hollow
moon
spills no grace

notes over tarred
rooftops
summer nights

plays no colors
on the
Empire State

If he is dead
how
may young men

hope to hear love's
lyrics
in each other

35

Dream Probe

What might it have meant—in the night, in the
strange depth of night—your fierce clasp
conjured thrusting my foot beneath the sheet
with a peremptory "there now"? Was it

some shadow quilted from scraps of day?
Was it—so tactile I waking feel fingers on my
ankle still—some subliminal communique?
You spoke of cats who, where you once

house sat, leapt into your dreams; was this
some like goad launched—assertive cat—
into my unguarded sleep? In pain the beauty
of it is that everything is rubbed fresh—like

sloughing off dead cells—and with that what
has clogged sensation: cut and lay back
sheaths of muscle; catch perception—oxygen
in a bottle; bleed ill men to health, well men

to immortality; gather delphinium on a cutting
basket, bittersweet as tangled thought
bewildered by the heady scent of peonies
unsettled as flights of breeze-blown flies.

Sounding

At times beneath the threshold of the ear—
Recurrent in that half-waking from sleep—
Sound is more felt than heard, at such a deep
Perception as to precipitate fear
That we might be about to fail a near,
Familiar voice—one we no longer keep
Beside us, but within—whose loss we weep,
Whose absent wisdom makes us strain to hear,
And to discern, messages from the dead.
Then reason intrudes: the whisper rises,
Resonates clearly as a car or plane;
Yet though the voice from our half-sleep has fled
It trails longing through memory's guises
To quicken intonations we sustain.

This Moment of June

Clouds cut like bloodless wounds
Through this moment of June—
This crispness after smothering,
Its lilt the conundrum of change—
This quiet moment in which we
Too often disappoint ourselves
Even as Nature (again) astounds:
Keats' little town forever still
Awaiting its bacchants' return;
A thrush call on the early mist;
The simile of sky breaking
Yellow over mountain rondeaus.
How dare one lag behind?
Caught up, buoyed on a breeze
Distilled in earth—still cool—we drift
Where we cannot be sought or
Hear haste's whispered urgencies.

In Cherry Blossom Light

Sometimes you're done before you even rise—Joe Bolton

We live a cultural imperative—though
To feel keenly is to twist the knife—
Which dictates stoic reserve even as we
Confront the vacant stare of noon:
I'm thinking of Lowell and Plath, Sexton
And Joe Bolton—"lost in my long alcohol"—
That chronicler of aimless dusks
And dawns before which hope has failed.
Strong tea turns brackish in the throat
And body starts to sense it's getting on
To check-out time from this motel—
And yet sometimes in cherry blossom light
My thought time travels to an innocence
When Greensheet-headlined "PEACE"
Sparked tears of joy, and summons up
The loss of the first boy I loved,
When I was eight. His name was Paul,
And I only knew the rush I felt—lungs
Full of brightness—when he showed up;
And even now I can see his face so
Clearly that I could number his freckles—
And the sharp glare in the schoolyard
That morning when he told me that
His family was leaving, moving north.
Spring comes, buds bloom, and so on;
Self-pity is the unforgivable.

Pronunciation Chart

1

at the front of the room
alone with apprehension
certain/uncertain in the moment
before my eyes rove
the pronunciation chart
so anxious for approval
from classmates' vacant eyes
no clue what they're thinking
or not thinking—
Sister Monica encouraging—
and not (yet) intimidated
not yet aware how unpopular
how threatening
knowledge could be

2

excused each morning
the following year
I tutored a classmate
in reading
we'd go to a reception parlor
(this was fourth grade)
the guy I tutored seemed
three times my size
wanted to joke around distract me
with sleight of hand tricks
whenever the principal
or another nun looked in
we'd plunge our heads
back of my neck and hands
would prick
hundreds of pins
until the nun passed on

3

abruptly the year before
Sister Monica had called me
to the front of the room
told me I'd been chosen
an altar boy—"no one
so young has ever been"—
I scared shitless (didn't know
the word)
walked the lonely walk
to church
we were paired told to keep
in vault-echo step
stained-glass light
off the tabernacle
awed me to drop a step
summary dismissal
Inconsolably I wept
my slow way back
mortified at failure
at how I'd bought myself
such shame

Vermont June

Stiff breeze harrows the unmown fields, ripe
For first cutting, cross-hatches foot trails
Into mountain clefts; the late sun warms
A patchwork of organ peals amid trees
Which stand out, each singular, distinct.
Light—spilt Frascati—freshens the palate,
Piques senses with unrivaled June: days—
Gifts—which in life have no equal, nowhere
Else such raspberry tang as suffuses
Sunset's softened air. Bats materialize
To sweep light's last follicles into barn
Corners of dusk; crickets chirrup transient
Joy, one season's life sufficient in flickers
Of fireflies which grace earth's first dark,
Canting like breeze-tossed lanterns, riding
Warmth to unhurried night, chasing children
Breathless to bed from their futile dashes
To snatch one last glimmer before day
Wraps itself into mountain burrows to be
Retrieved only in bright-etched morning.

Peter McNamara grew up in Vermont and spends part of each year at his Danby home. *like a perhaps hand* is his third poetry collection (St. Andrews Press published **Loneliness of the Palm** in 1993). For the composer Dean X. Johnson, he wrote choral lyrics and a libretto for **The Great Bridge**, an opera performed during the Brooklyn Bridge Centennial.

He taught at Georgetown University, The University of North Carolina at Chapel Hill, and several prep schools, and now gives occasional poetry workshops. He was named Ronald H. Bayes Writer-in-Residence at St. Andrews Presbyterian College for Spring Term 2000.